GW01236559

Postman Pat's Day in Bed

Story by John Cunliffe
Pictures by Joan Hickson

From the original Television designs by Ivor Wood

André Deutsch/Hippo Books

Published simultaneously in hardback by
André Deutsch Limited,
105-106 Great Russell Street, London WC1B 3LJ
and in paperback by Hippo Books, Scholastic Publications Limited,
10 Earlham Street, London WC2H 9RX in 1987

Text copyright © 1987 John Cunliffe
Illustrations copyright © 1987 by André Deutsch Limited,
Scholastic Publications Limited
and Woodland Animations Limited

All rights reserved

ISBN 0 233 98120 9 (hardback)
ISBN 0 590 70737 X (paperback)

Made and printed in Belgium by Proost
Typeset in Plantin by Span Graphics, London

This book is sold subject to the condition that it shall not, by way of trade
or otherwise, be lent, re-sold, hired out, or otherwise circulated without
the publisher's prior consent in any form of binding or cover other than
that in which it is published and without a similar condition including this
condition being imposed on the subsequent purchaser.

Pat woke up.

"Oh! Ouch!"

He felt bad.

He felt really bad.

His head hurt.

His nose was sore.

His throat was sore.

He sneezed and sneezed again.

He tried to get out of bed.
"Oh dear! Ooooh, my head!"
Poor Pat! His head hurt more than ever.
He flopped back into bed.
Jess came to see what was wrong.
"Hello, Jess," said Pat. "I can't get up today. I think I've got 'flu."
Jess licked Pat's hand to cheer him up.
"You'll have to take my letters, today, Jess," said Pat.

But Jess curled up at the end of the bed and went to sleep.

"Never mind, I'll ring Pencaster," said Pat, "and tell them I'm poorly. I expect they'll send Jim. He's been before."

"Jim's on holiday," said the man in Pencaster. "We'll send Mollie."

"I don't know Mollie," said Pat. "She must be new."

Then he went back to sleep.

When Pat woke up he was feeling a bit better.

Pat didn't like staying in bed. He wanted to be out and about, chatting with all his friends in Greendale. Oh, how he hated it!

"I wonder how Mollie's getting on," said Pat. "She's sure to get lost. She doesn't know Greendale at all."

There was a ring at the door.

"Come in!" called Pat.

Mrs. Goggins put her head round the
bedroom door.
"Hello, Pat! They rang from
Pencaster to say you were poorly.
Dear me, I think you've got 'flu.
Never mind, I won't catch it; I had it
a while back. I've brought you the
paper, and don't you worry about the
letters. Mollie's taking good care of them.

Now you stay warm in bed,
and I'll get you a nice hot drink and
an aspirin, and you'll soon feel
better."

Pat had his drink and aspirin.

Jess had a saucer of milk.

Pat felt a bit better.

Mrs. Goggins put a thermos of hot coffee by the bedside.

"That'll keep you going when you feel thirsty," she said. "I'll have to go and see to the shop now, but I'll give the doctor a ring, and ask her to pop in to see you."

Pat and Jess had a good sleep.
Later on, Pat sat up in bed and read the paper.

That cheered him up.
Pat heard the "ping" of a bicycle-bell outside, then another ring at the door. Here was Miss Hubbard, come to see Pat.

"Hello, Pat. I heard you were in bed with 'flu. I've brought you a bottle of my best nettle wine. That'll soon have you on your feet. Don't worry about the letters. There's a lovely post-lady delivering them."

Pat sat up in bed and had a glass of nettle wine.

He felt much better.

On the way to Thompson Ground, Mollie had taken a wrong turning, on to a muddy track. Her wheels had stuck in the mud, and Peter Fogg was pulling her out with his tractor.

Mollie didn't worry. She just laughed.
"It's great here. Just great!"
She loved being in Greendale. It made a nice change from the town.

When she got to Thompson Ground at last, Dorothy was baking. She gave Mollie a big slice of fruitcake and a cup of tea.

"This is a great life," said Mollie. "Does this happen every day?"

"Most days," said Dorothy. "It's nothing special. I'll bake an extra cake for Pat."

Alf showed Mollie the new chicks in the barn. She loved them.

Mollie was on her way.

She stopped to watch the lambs playing in the fields.

She stopped to listen to the birds singing.

She stopped to see the piglets at Greendale Farm.

She stroked a foal at Hill Top.
"I'll never get the letters delivered at this rate," she said. "There's so much to see."
Mollie was very late with the letters, but she was so happy and cheerful that no one seemed to mind.

When she called on Ted Glen, he mended her broken watch-strap. She ordered a pair of shoes from Granny Dryden's catalogue.

At the school, she sat down and told the children a story about Anansi the spider. They loved her.

When she met Sam in his mobile-shop, she bought some sandwiches and a can of fruit juice.

"Where's Pat?" everyone said.

"Don't worry," said Mollie. "He'll soon be back."

Pat was having a busy time, too. Dorothy Thompson called with a cake.

The Reverend Timms brought the parish magazine and a bunch of grapes.

Ted Glen brought a puzzle he'd made out of wood. Pat couldn't do it, no matter how he tried.

Granny Dryden brought some herb tea.

Sam Waldron brought a bunch of bananas.
Jess brought a toy mouse from his basket.
Peter Fogg brought a crossword book.

Dr. Gilbertson brought two books and a bottle of brown medicine. She took his temperature, and felt his pulse. "You must stay off work till Tuesday," she said. "Then you'll be as right as rain."

Katy and Tom called after school, with a picture of Anansi and a packet of sweets.

Last of all, Mollie came, with two letters for Pat.

"Thanks for doing my work," said Pat. "I'm sorry to be such a bother."

"Bother?" said Mollie. "Bother? It's no bother! I love it here."

"Dr. Gilbertson says I have to stay off work till next Tuesday," said Pat.

"A whole week!" said Mollie, grinning. "Great! Can't you make it two weeks? I just love it here."

She told Pat about all her adventures in Greendale. He felt much better.

He was soon allowed out of bed, but he couldn't go out.

The day came at last when he could get his red van out again, and set off with the letters.

It was a happy day for Pat, but a sad day for Mollie. She didn't want to go back to the town.

Then, one day in September, the post office telephone rang.

"It's for you, Pat," said Mrs. Goggins. And who do you think it was? It was Mollie, of course.

"Hey, Pat," she said, "what do you think? I have a new job!"

"Where is it?" said Pat.

"Langdale!"

"Great!" said Pat.

"It is," said Mollie. "It certainly is. And what do you think? Dorothy Thompson's sister lives here, and her cakes are even nicer than Dorothy's."

"Give me a ring, if you get 'flu," said Pat, with a smile.